E.M.C.E.
The Ohio State University at Newark
University Drive
Newark, Ohio 43055

MALTA

MALTA

ROGER BALM
Rutgers University

THE AMERICAN GEOGRAPHICAL SOCIETY

Around the World Program

HILARY LAMBERT HOPPER
University of Kentucky
Series Editor

The McDonald & Woodward Publishing Company
Blacksburg, Virginia
1995

The McDonald & Woodward Publishing Company
P. O. Box 10308, Blacksburg, Virginia 24062-0308

THE AMERICAN GEOGRAPHICAL SOCIETY
Around the World Program

Malta

© 1995 by The American Geographical Society
The American Geographical Society is the oldest professional geographical society in the United States and a recognized pioneer in geographical research and education.

All rights reserved. First printing, 1995
Composition by Rowan Mountain, Inc., Blacksburg, Virginia
Printed in Canada by Friesen Printers, Altona, Manitoba

01 00 99 98 97 96 95   10 9 8 7 6 5 4 3 2 1

Library of Congress Cataloging-in-Publication Data

Balm, Roger, 1947–
    Malta / Roger Balm.
        p.   cm. — (The American Geographical Society Around the World Program)
        Includes bibliographical references.
        ISBN 0-939923-58-0 (lib. bdg :alk. paper). — ISBN 0-939923-57-2 (pbk. : alk. paper)
        1. Malta. I. Title. II. Series: American Geographical Society Around the World Program (Series)
DG989.B25 1995
914.58'5—dc20   95-42380
                                                                                                                    CIP

Acknowledgements: The author is grateful for the assistance of the National Tourism Organisation of Malta and the Foundation for International Studies, Valletta, for providing supporting photographs and information. Briavel Holcomb initiated the idea for this contribution to the Around the World Program and, through her enthusiasm, ensured its completion.

Cover: Brightly colored fishing boats — *luzzus* — are distinctive elements of the Maltese landscape. Most *luzzus* are made of imported cedar; the fresh paint protects a valuable investment while the Eye of Osiris protects the crew of the boat. This photo was taken at Marsaxlokk, on the southeastern coast of Malta, by Roger Balm.

Original sketches: Roger Balm (pp. 12, 21); Jennifer Snow (pp. i, 20, 37, 49)

Photo credits: Roger Balm (pp. 7, 10, 14, 16, 24, 30, 36, 39 top, 44, 51, 53); Ralph E. Eshelman (pp. 27, 34, 39 bottom); National Tourism Organisation of Malta (pp. 2, 8, 18, 28, 42, 50, 57).
Mountain High Maps images on p. iv and back cover © 1993 Digital Wisdom, Inc.

Reproduction or translation of any part of this work, except for short excerpts used in reviews, without the written permission of The American Geographical Society is unlawful. Requests for permission to reproduce parts of this work should be addressed to The American Geographical Society, 156 Fifth Avenue, Suite 600, New York, New York 10010.

For additional information about the Around the World Program, please contact the publisher.

TABLE OF CONTENTS

14°34′E
36°05′N

GOZO
(Ghawdex)

Fungus
Rock
Ghasri
Qawra
Xaghra
Victoria
Xlendi
Mgarr

COMINO

COMINOTTO

Marfa Point

Saint Pauls
Islands
Saint Pauls Bay
Salina Bay

Mediterranean
Sea

Bugibba

Victoria
Lines
Naxxar
Saint Julians Bay
Mosta
Sliema
Marsamxett Harbor
Tigné
Mdina
Attard
Floriana
Rabat
Hamrun
Buskett
Paola
Dingli
Luqa
Saint Angelo
Valletta
Grand
Harbor
Fort

N

0   5 Miles
0   7 Kilometers

MALTA
Ghar Lapsi
Marsaxlokk
Malta Freeport
Delimara
Point
FILFLA
Pretty Saint Georges
Bay   Bay

35°49′N
14°12′E

The Maltese Islands and their place in the Mediterranean Sea.
Only the islands of Malta, Gozo, and Comino are inhabited by humans at this time.

MALTA

MALTA

Although many geographers and seasoned travelers claim that the best way to approach islands is by sea, for Malta the best approach is by air. When flying to Malta in fair weather, the first sight of the Maltese Islands comes as a shock. The archipelago is centrally located in the Mediterranean Sea between Italy and the coast of North Africa and, after the relative emptiness of island neighbors encountered en route, such as Sardinia, Sicily, and Corsica, the closely packed Maltese towns and villages resemble a roughly daubed stucco troweled onto the land. There is little in this landscape that has not been formed by the human hand and, from our window seat, the meticulous terracing of the fields to conserve the scarce soil, and the subdivision of the fields into tiny plots, are particularly striking. To see the huge stone quarries from the air is to realize that these islands have been turned inside out in order for their towns to grow.

Victoria, the largest city on the island of Gozo, from the air. The golden tone of the built landscape, the mixture of European and African influences on architecture and land use, and the widespread evidence of human modification of the land are clearly shown.

To find a suitable metaphor for the Maltese people one need look no further than this soft limestone rock of which the islands are largely composed. It is still the material of choice for many Maltese buildings and has the remarkable quality of toughening over time and gaining strength with age. So, by necessity, these island people have developed toughness and strength, not only to compensate for the islands' lack of natural resources, but also to adjust to the many invaders and occupiers that history has brought to these most strategically valuable of Mediterranean islands.

The Romans called Malta *Melita,* from the Greek word *meli* meaning "honey," and some claim that is how Malta gained its name. Certainly Malta has long had a reputation for producing fine honey. But so much about the islands also has a golden brown color about it — the fresh cut stone from the quarries, the parched fields of summer, the crusty bread fresh from the bakers' ovens. Even the late afternoon sun sets gleaming the stone churches that everywhere punctuate the landscape. A less poetic but more plausible origin of the name Malta can be traced back to the Phoenician settlement of the islands about 700 BC. These early colonizers named the place *Maleth,* meaning "place of shelter," "haven," or "hiding place." Malta has frequently been all three of these, boasting as it does one of the finest natural harbors in the world.

Taken together, the islands of Malta have an area of 122 square miles which is about twice that of Washington DC, or about one-tenth the size of Rhode Island, the smallest state in the United States. No town or village on Malta Island, the main island, is more than an hour's bus ride from Valletta, the nation's capital. On Gozo, the smaller neighbor to the west of Malta Island, the centrally located town of Victoria is similarly within easy reach of outlying villages. In part because of its size, Malta is one of the most densely populated nations on earth and, looking upon these islands from the air, one can sense the challenges that confront this small island nation as it moves into the European mainstream of development and social change, while accommodating the needs of an increasingly prosperous people. Looking down, we become aware of the human inventiveness that has transformed the Maltese landscape over millennia in order to coax sustenance from the poor soils and to make the most of scarce water supplies. From above, in short, can be seen a landscape of resourcefulness in a place of few resources.

But setting aside the thought-provoking views of Malta from the air, it is the Malta at ground level that this book is about. Talk to people about twentieth century realities of life on small islands that are tourist magnets and those people quickly fall into two groups: the pessimists who believe that the rising tide of commercialism is sweeping away traditional culture, and the optimists who believe the roots of the past run deep and hold fast despite rapid change. As you read this book you will see that, as a geographer, the author doesn't belong with either group. Malta is a small island nation determined to find a secure future free from the boom-and-bust economics to which much of its military history condemned it. In fashioning that future, some troubling compromises and sacrifices have been made. But the Maltese sense of kinship, generosity, and identity endures, and these essential ingredients of life will linger in some form no matter what the future brings.

POPULATION DENSITY OF ISLAND NATIONS
PEOPLE PER SQUARE MILE

Country	Density	Country	Density
Singapore	11,205	Comoros	513
Malta	**2,792**	Dominican Republic	367
Barbados	1,533	Cuba	243
Mauritius	1,467	Cape Verde	226
Japan	842	Cyprus	192
Sri Lanka	663	Ireland	134
Trinidad & Tobago	627	Madagascar	50
United Kingdom	611	Solomon Islands	29
Haiti	588	Papua New Guinea	22
Jamaica	581	Iceland	6
Phillipines	518		

Source: United Nations Statistical Office.

A LAND RICH

IN EVERYTHING THAT IS GOOD

The Maltese archipelago is located sixty miles south of Sicily and one-hundred-eighty miles north of the Tunisian coast of North Africa between latitude 35° 48' 28" and 36° 05' 00" north and longitude 14° 11' 04" and 14° 34' 37" east. Only the three largest islands of the group are inhabited today: Malta, with an area of 94.9 square miles, and by far the largest of the group; Gozo (in Maltese *Ghawdex*); and Comino (*Kemmuna*). The uninhabited islets are Comminotto (*Kemmunett*); Saint Pauls Islands (*Il-Gzejjer ta' San Pawl*) where, according to the Bible, the Apostle Paul was shipwrecked; Fungus Rock (*Il-Hagra tal-General*), once prized for the medicinal powers of its cliff-top vegetation; and an outlying island to the south of Malta, long used for bombing practice, which is still known by its Maltese name of Filfla.

If the Mediterranean were drained of its waters, the Maltese Islands would be seen to occupy a ridge extending from the Ragusa Peninsula of Sicily south towards the African coast. Known as the Hyblean Plateau, this ridge divides the Mediterranean Sea into its two basins. This ridge is now deeply submerged but was above sea level far back in geological time. We know this because in some Maltese caves, such as those at Ghar Dalam, fossil remains have been found. These include pygmy elephants, hippopotamuses, and giant tortoises that lumbered and crawled over this transcontinental bridge between Africa and Eurasia. Based on the fossils that have been found, we know that climatic conditions during parts of the Pleistocene epoch, between about 1.6 million and ten thousand years ago, must have been considerably wetter, and the vegetation much more lush, than today to support these exotic animals.

The rocks of the Maltese Islands are arranged in the form of a giant sandwich. The "bread" is a hard coralline limestone, the oldest of which dates to

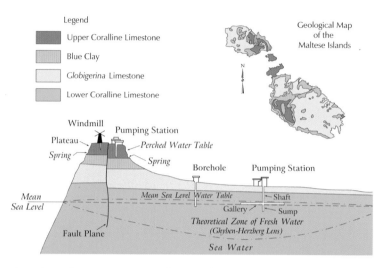

A geological section across Malta, southwest (left) to northeast (right),
showing the different layers of rocks that make up the island
and the position of fresh water sources.

the Tertiary period of about thirty million years ago. The "filling" consists of softer rocks of globigerina limestone, interlayered with blue clay and greensand. All the rocks we see in Malta were originally formed under water. Walk the quiet roads that border the fields of western Malta and you are walking on coral, and a close look will reveal the remains of ancient sea life now turned to stone and lifted from the sea bed. Look out from the high cliffs south of the Dingli Plateau to the adjacent headlands and you will clearly see the layers of the rocks exposed in the order in which their sediments were first deposited those millions of years ago. Yet even these spectacular limestone cliffs are just the topmost portion of limestone rocks that extend down more than nine thousand feet.

The twenty-minute trip on the ferry boat between Marfa Point on the western end of Malta and Mgarr on Gozo takes one close by the island of Comino. Here and there are archways where the limestone has been punched through by the waves of the Mediterranean. Underwater caves, a great fascination to divers, are also found here. From the ferry, one can often see clear to the bottom of the shallow waters which glows turquoise as the sunlight is reflected from the underwater limestone shelves. True beaches, however, are scarce in the Maltese Islands because the limestone rocks do not readily break down into sand.

Much of the main island is often described as undulating countryside. Such general descriptions are subjective though, and anyone who has climbed Saqqajja Hill to Mdina en route to a hotel room after a day exploring on foot or by bicycle would certainly not agree! This old town, once the capital of Malta, occupies the high ground of a south-central plateau. Traveling south from there, the land slopes down before dropping precipitously to sea level at the Dingli Cliffs. In Gozo, the landscape is also punctu-

ated by many flat-topped plateaux. Here, as on the main island, the shape of the land has influenced the location and form of the towns, with the most favored sites for towns being on high ground in the interior from where it was easier to detect pirates and invaders.

As in many places in the Mediterranean region, the Maltese Islands have been molded by the gradual pushing, pulling, and colliding that result from the movement of the earth's crust, a process known as plate tectonics. Tectonic forces have tilted Malta Island so that the surface dips to the northeast like a table with two legs shorter than the others. The steep cliffs of the southern coast rise to nearly nine hundred feet, giving this region the highest

Some of the rock types that make up Malta are exposed at the Dingli Cliffs along the south side of Malta.

ground in Malta, while on the other side of the island there are drowned valleys along the flanks of which now stands the capital city of Valletta. It is the depth and straightness of these drowned valleys that enable today's cruise ships and oil tankers to enter Malta's Grand Harbor and adjacent

The Azure Window on Gozo, a picturesque example of coastal erosion.

creeks to find a secure and sheltered berth.

These same tectonic forces have twisted and broken the rocks of Malta over the course of the last fifteen million years. In the western part of the main island, for example, in the vicinity of the Victoria Lines, are fault lines where the land surface has been dislo-

cated by tectonic forces to form high ridges alternating with narrow flat-bottomed valleys, geological structures known as horsts and grabens, respectively. The valleys where streams flow intermittently are called *widien* by the Maltese; the most fertile agricultural land often is found in such places. A less benign aspect of the tectonic character of this part of the Mediterranean is the risk of earthquakes. The last serious earthquake was in 1693 when Mdina, then the capital of Malta, was virtually destroyed, and Rabat (now Victoria), on Gozo, was also badly affected. Some of the rubble from this earthquake can still be seen on Gozo today.

More than ten thousand years ago, before the first human settlers arrived, the harsh light of Malta's Mediterranean summer would have been filtered by a forest containing Holm oak

(*Quercus ilex*) and Aleppo pine (*Pinus halepensis*). With the exception of scattered citrus and olive groves, and the carefully protected grove at Buskett, near the inland town of Rabat, trees are now scarce in Malta. Many olive and citrus trees were removed as recently as the nineteenth century to make way for the planting of cotton. Though trees may be scarce, cactus is abundant in the form of prickly pear (*Opuntia ficus indica*). Though a relative newcomer to the island, these spiny plants with their leathery leaves big as baseball mitts find the Maltese soils and climate ideal, and prickly pear now seems to hang over every wall, especially in rural Malta where it is often used as a living hedge in conjunction with the stone walls.

An Arab text from the ninth century AD proclaimed "Malitah...rich in everything that is good and in the blessing of God." But much damage to this fragile land had probably already occurred. Trees were felled by early settlers for fuel, building materials, or to clear the land for crops and for grazing animals. Since these animals would nibble the shoots of any trees attempting to re-grow, no regeneration was possible. With the trees went the best of Malta's soils. Writers of antiquity described the blood-red of the streams as it carried away the soils from mainland Italy, and so it must have been in Malta under the force of the often harsh winter rains. Strong winds, too, would have blown away soil exposed on ridges and upper slopes. But some relict soils, sometimes described as *terra rossa*, remain and these are usually associated with the pockets of blue clay mentioned earlier. Such soils are particularly evident on Gozo. Walk across to northwestern Gozo and we will see, enclosed with rubble limestone walls in the traditional Maltese style, soils of such a rich, warm brown that they appear to have been mixed on an artist's palette. So it is that the best Maltese vegetables ripen in the most ancient of its soils.

Though the people of Gozo are quick to point out the superior fertility of their fields and the greater depth of soil, not until millennia to come, when the Maltese Islands might again have a less seasonal and erratic rainfall, will fertile soil be naturally created here.

And not until then will the Maltese finally be relieved of their age-old nemesis: drought. Average annual rainfall is 20.54 inches, slightly more than the average found in the vicinity of the one-hundredth meridian on the North American Great Plains. But here in the Mediterranean, unlike in the central United States, almost all the rain falls in the winter months between October and March. In addition, there can be extreme variability from year to year and, since records began, there are few months that have not been times of complete drought. Even after the heavy showers of winter, few Maltese streams flow for more than a few hours because much of the rain percolates underground through the rock.

After ducking into the nearest cafe to avoid a torrential winter downpour of rain and hailstones, it is hard to believe that only sixteen to twenty-five percent of rainfall flows down through the limestone bedrock to replenish the groundwater aquifers. The water that does infiltrate trickles slowly through the semi-porous limestone much as water passes through a sponge. Since Malta is a small island, the rainwater can only seep down so far into the rock "sponge" before it encounters seawater. Less dense than the seawater, the rainwater, now far underground, floats on top of the seawater in the form of a dome-shaped reservoir referred to by hydrologists as a "lens." It is from this lens that a substantial portion of Malta's water is drawn.

Undoubtedly the time of greatest

Winding limestone walls and red soils dominate this view of rural Malta's agricultural landscape. Note the prickly pear cactus in the foreground.

water need is the summer when the skies are cloudless, the temperature rises to near 90°F every day, and even the skimpiest of cooling shadows seem impossible to find. While it is true that plants need abundant sunshine in order to thrive, they also need moisture. With a favorable soil-moisture balance, the vegetation of Malta would be luxuriant, but as it is, the soil moisture declines so much in the dry months that the summer is a time when many plants are dormant. Unless, of course, some form of irrigation is used — which is not possible in Malta because of water scarcity. When traveling in Malta, look up at the roof tops and notice the rain-trapping cisterns on almost every building; notice also the tanks and pipes in the farmers' fields. Even the runoff from roads is often channeled down to the fields through gutters.

The clear skies of summer stem from the dominance of the Azores high pressure system which moves north and east of its wintertime position over the eastern Atlantic Ocean. Meteorologists associate high pressure with calm winds and sunny skies, and certainly Malta receives a great deal of sunshine with a year-round average of 8.3 hours per day. The islands are also very windy with only eight percent of days being recorded as calm. Indeed, it is often the winds which serve as the most potent reminder of Malta's geographic situation. The *xlokk*, a wind notorious for its debilitating effect on plants and people alike, occasionally blows north from the Sahara Desert in northern Africa. This wind displaces the more usual northwesterly flow of air and occasionally deposits a thin film of desert sand on the islands. Also distinguished by name is the fierce northeasterly wind of the winter months, known as the *grigale*, that blows across from the Adriatic Sea; even the fine natural harbors of Valletta can be disturbed by this powerful wind. Square-rigged and unable to sail to windward, could the ship that carried Paul the Apostle have been wrecked by the *grigale*? We can only speculate about this event that changed forever the cultural geography of Malta.

BLOOD AND STONE

Some say that from the high ground beyond Cape Passero in southeastern Sicily, the Maltese Islands, sixty miles away, can be seen on a clear day. There is little doubt that the first Maltese came from Sicily, but their first encounter with the islands may well have been by chance. In any event, the settlers of five thousand to seven thousand years ago would have come to a place that was considerably greener and more lush than it is today. Almost

certainly these settlers would have brought with them in their boats grain and some domestic animals.

Archaeologists have found evidence of Neolithic cave dwellers on Malta that date to 3800 BC. Many of Malta's first settlers were also skilled architects and masons and exploited to the full the abundant stone beneath their feet. At least twenty groups of temples that were erected between 3500 and 2500 BC have survived to the present day. Particularly notable are the temple at Tarxien with its five apses and precisely fitted blocks, Mnajdra with its corbeled walls and cliff-top views out towards the island of Filfla, and Hagar Qim where several carved figurines of "mother goddesses" have been unearthed. These are sometimes known as "fat divinities" since they depict obese women and may have been some

The Venus of Malta, *a goddess figurine from Hagar Qim.*

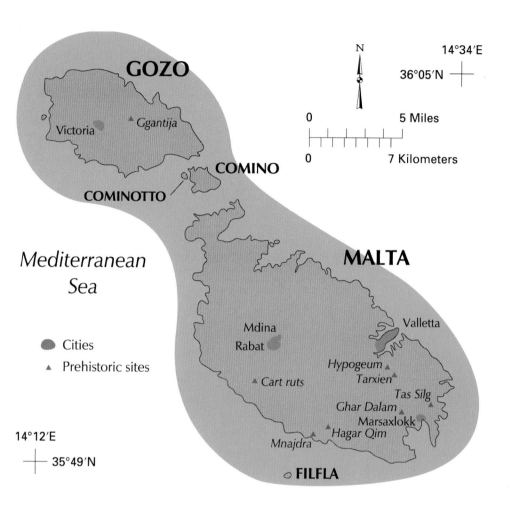

Prehistoric sites on the Maltese Islands mentioned in the text.

form of fertility symbol. These early builders not only constructed buildings above ground but also impressive underground mausoleums such as the Hypogeum, near the present-day town of Paola; its system of caves, cubicles and passageways dates to about 2400 BC and may at one time have held as many as seven thousand bodies.

Such structures as these are all the more remarkable for having been hewn with picks and axes made from bone and flint, since metal tools were unknown in the Maltese Islands until the

Ggantija Temple on Gozo, one of the earlier prehistoric temples built on the Maltese Islands.

period 2500–1500 BC. All the free-standing buildings also required the quarrying and moving of immense loads of stone. Clearly visible in an area near the Dingli Cliffs are "cart ruts" worn in the limestone with grooves running with the regularity of railroad tracks, and it is thought these may have been caused by the repetitive hauling of stone-bearing sledges or primitive wheeled carts from quarry face to roadway.

If the prehistoric settlers first glimpsed Malta across the water from high ground, the Phoenicians, who had arrived by 700 BC, almost certainly sighted the islands from sea level. The trans-Mediterranean trade route between Phoenicia — the lands surrounding present-day Tyre and Sidon — and Carthage in North Africa was

long and dangerous, so Malta would have been a welcome port-of-call, as it has long remained for mariners down to the present day. In addition to the archaic pottery the Phoenicians left behind, some claim that the roots of the Maltese language, a rare tongue little heard outside of the islands, can be traced to the Phoenicians.

As Carthage prospered, the role of Malta as an important military and political outpost grew. By the middle of the sixth century BC, Malta had been endowed with a strategic military value that would endure until the end of World War II, more than two thousand years later. The Carthaginians built several important temples in the islands, including the recently excavated Tas Silg. In addition to the ties with Carthage and the Punic culture, com-

THE MALTESE LANGUAGE — A LIVING RELIC

The biblical account in the *Acts of the Apostles* of Paul's shipwreck in AD 60 describes the islanders as *Barbaroi*, a disparaging term reserved for those who spoke neither Latin nor Greek. If not Latin or Greek, could the language have been a form of Phoenician? It has been claimed that Phoenician was still being spoken at the time of the arrival in the islands of the Arabs from Sicily in AD 870 and that was why the local language was so readily understandable by Malta's new rulers. Today's visitors from Malta's neighboring Arab countries are able to understand a considerable number of spoken words. *Halib,* for example, is common to both as the word for milk. *Malti* is a Semitic language and, as far as we know today, about seventy-five percent of its word forms have evolved from spoken Phoenician, with the rest being of Romance origin. *Malti* is, however, the only Semitic tongue that is written in Latin script.

Most of the place names to be found on a map of Malta are Arabic in origin and are a good way to start learning Maltese pronunciation. Town names incorporating the word *marsa* (such as Marsaxlokk) are fairly easy because *marsa* means "harbor" in *Malti*. The word *wied* is also a good clue since it means "valley." When speaking the word, emphasize the syllable in italics.

Mgarr	Im-*jar*	Luqa	*Loo*-hah
Xaghra	*Shar*-uh	Xlendi	Sh-*len*-dee
Ghasri	*Arsh*-ree	Qawra	*Ow*-rah
Marsaxlokk	*Mar*-sah-shlock	Naxxar	*Narsh*-ah
Mdina	Im-*dee*-nah	Ghawdex	*Ow*-desh
Zurrieq	Soo-ree-*ek*		

mercial links were established with the Greek cities on Sicily, an island then known to the Greeks as *Magna Graecia*. From the fourth century BC, the power of Rome in southern Italy increased and came into conflict with that of Carthage. Hostilities quickly turned into a struggle-to-the-death of two great powers. Caught between the two sides was tiny Malta, which fell to Rome in 218 BC, and remained under Roman administration for over a thousand years.

Though the time of Roman administration was one of relative prosperity, the extent to which Malta fell fully under the influence of the Romans is questionable. Certainly the Romans applied a strong administrative hand and many fine artifacts were left behind by the occupiers. A stroll today around the ancient city of Mdina and the adjoining town of Rabat will eventually take you past a reconstructed Roman villa now used as a museum.

It was in AD 60 while Malta was under Roman rule that the islands' most distinguished visitor inadvertently came to call. In that year, a ship with 275 passengers aboard, including the Apostle Paul, was caught in a fierce

Today, looking out seaward from the tourist-besieged town of Bugibba, one can see the Saint Pauls Islands and the monument commemorating the apostle's landing.

The issue of faith in Malta was closely tied to the identity of the islands' occupiers. Following the so-called Dark Ages, about which little is known regarding the islands' history, the Arabs took control of Malta in AD

Beyond the remains of an abandoned fishing boat one can see the Saint Pauls Islands and Saint Pauls Bay. The Apostle Paul was shipwrecked on this coast in AD 60.

storm and wrecked on the northern shore of the main island. According to the biblical account Paul was shown "no little kindness" and he remained on the island for three months living in a limestone grotto in the town of Rabat. By all accounts his stay was influential for Malta was one of the first Roman colonies to become Christian.

870, adding them to their geographic realm that included much of present-day Spain, France, and Italy. The language being spoken in Malta at that time would have sounded familiar to them, but much else in Malta had to be refashioned to their taste. The Arabs introduced the growing of cotton and citrus and left a distinctive architectural mark on Malta's then-capital, Mdina. By reducing the size of the town, Malta's new occupiers felt the capital could be better defended. Today, the entry into Mdina is still via one of two gates through massive stone walls, inside of which is a maze of alleyways and small squares. The population of Mdina is fewer than 500 and, although restrictions against the entry of cars have unfortunately been relaxed in recent years, Mdina still deserves its title of the "Silent City."

The invading forces of Roger the Norman arrived from Sicily in 1090 and ended Arab rule, but the Moslem influence remained strong. As late as the middle of the thirteenth century Moslems were still in the majority and controlled most of Malta's wealth, but by late in that century the Christian cathedral in Mdina was providing a range of religious services and Malta was falling increasingly under the influence of Europe. However, lying as it did at the frontier between competing faiths, the struggle for dominance was far from over for Malta.

In 1530, the Maltese Islands were ceded by the Holy Roman Emperor,

Charles V of Spain, to the Knights Hospitallers of Saint John of Jerusalem. The Knights had been driven from their base in Rhodes by the Turks in 1523, and had somewhat reluctantly chosen to establish themselves in Malta. The Knights were a charitable holy order whose members were drawn from the ranks of the European nobility. They were not averse to using the sword and the cannon in defense of their territory and causes, principal among which was to repel the spread of Islam in Europe. The yearly rent for the fortress island of Malta that the Knights would create was one falcon, payable to the King of Spain on All Saints' Day. (The movie *The Maltese Falcon* draws its title from this piece of history but otherwise is complete fiction.)

The Knights turned out to be the most determined builders the islands had known since the temple-builders of old. Valletta, with its distinctive rectilinear street pattern, was laid out by them on the heights of Mount Scibberas and named after a Grand Master of the Knights — Jean de la Valette. To distinguish the new capital

from the old, the Knights dubbed Mdina *Città Vecchia*, or "Old City." Within the new city of Valletta, gracious town homes, known as *auberges*, were constructed so that Knights drawn from each of the eight nationalities within the Order at that time might live together.

In many ways, by transforming Malta into a fortress, the Knights laid the foundation for all of Malta's later history. Malta's military value could only be fully realized through the massive capital spending and engineering works that the Knights were prepared to underwrite. The influence of the Knights on the Maltese landscape was not limited just to the area around Valletta. Their reign brought considerable prosperity to the Maltese and with it an increase in population and expansion in size of many island towns and villages. Still evident today is the heavy investment that the Knights made in the water-supply infrastructure to protect against the perils of drought. Extending through the present-day Valletta suburbs of Attard and Hamrun are the well-preserved remains of an aqueduct. Although no longer used today, when it was constructed between 1610 and 1614 it carried well-water by gravity several miles from the center of the island to the urban areas around the harbor.

Not content with forcing the Knights from Rhodes, the Turks made frequent raids on the Maltese Islands in the 1550s. During one attack, they carried off into slavery virtually the entire population of Gozo. The Knights knew that their old enemies the Turks would eventually seek their total defeat in battle, and on virtually every headland on Malta and Gozo, but especially along the northern coast of the main island, their watch towers can be seen still casting a stony eye seaward to gain early warning of an invasion. Many of the massive walls that can be seen today in the vicinity of Fort Saint Angelo, near Valletta, held at bay the Turks who, fighting for Süleyman the Magnificent and the cause of Islam,

Valletta, built by the Knights as their new capital, from the air. The Triton Fountain and bus terminal are in the foreground and Fort Saint Elmo is in the distance.

eventually stormed ashore at Marsaxlokk in 1565.

Whether or not it is true that the heads of Malta's Turkish invaders were used as cannonballs, and the bodies of its Christian defenders were lashed to wooden crosses and floated headless across the creeks, the stirring times of the mid-sixteenth century that culminated in the Great Siege are as vivid in the minds of many Maltese today as if they occurred yesterday. From May until October of 1565, the Knights fought back the assaults. As the bodies piled high below the Knights' defenses through the Mediterranean summer, Malta's defenders maintained hope that reinforcements would arrive from Sicily. When eventually relief came and the siege was lifted, the force of seven hundred Knights and three thousand Maltese troops had been reduced to six hundred near-starving defenders. All things considered, the Turks should have defeated the Knights since they had greater numbers and were skilled military tacticians. The compelling belief on the part of the Knights that courage and honor were all-important, however, maintained their spirits and

finally carried the day. September 8, the day on which the Great Siege is said to have been ended, is now celebrated as an important public holiday in Malta — the Feast of Our Lady of Victories. And despite the passing of centuries, the Order of the Knights of Saint John is still in existence. Although the Order left Malta in 1798, it maintains a headquarters in Rome.

The pervasive memory of the Knights' tenure is best symbolized by

The imprint of the Knights on the cultural landscape of Malta has been vast and enduring.

Medieval and Baroque architecture in Mdina.

the eight-pointed Maltese Cross, which they brought to the island. Wherever one looks in Malta today there seems to be a Maltese Cross — carved into the prows of fishing boats and into stone steps, welded into wrought-iron gates, worked into the filigree earrings for sale in the gift shops, sewn into the patterns of the traditional lacework. It even emblazons the tailplanes of the Air Malta passenger jets.

The Knights' long tenure came to an end in 1798, hastened by the actions of the French who confiscated much of the Knights' property in France and generally restricted financial support of the Order. As a result of the Knights' vulnerability and pro-French sentiment within Malta itself, the Order surrendered to the forces of Napoleon. The occupation by the French from 1798 to 1800 eventually provoked revolt by the Maltese who were outraged by the looting and vandalizing of the islands' churches and the purging of its clergy by Napoleon's army. Quick to seize the advantage, British naval commanders dispatched a fleet of vessels to the is-

THE KNIGHTS OF MALTA TODAY

The Knights of Saint John governed Malta for over two-hundred-fifty years, and in the armory building in Valletta one can see their helmets and steel tunics. Though the suits of armor have long been unworn and now belong only in a museum, the Order of Saint John remains active today. In Malta itself there are about three dozen members, most of them elderly, though worldwide membership of the Order is about 9,600, including about 1,500 in the United States. Only Europeans of long-standing nobility can reach positions of leadership within the Order.

The Knights' original mission was to care for the sick and wounded during the twelfth century crusades, hence their other name "hospitallers." A tradition of nursing the ill has been carried down to the present day. In Malta, the Knights maintain an important blood bank for the islands' people. In England, the Saint John Ambulance Brigade is well known for its skilled provision of first aid and comfort during times of crisis, and the Brigade's uniform still features the eight-pointed Maltese Cross.

Today, the Sovereign Military Order of Malta is based in Rome and is officially the world's smallest country, with an area equivalent to about half a football field. It is also the only country with a street address (68, Via Condotti), the only one completely surrounded by a wall, and the only one without citizens since all members of the Order retain their own nationality. Archives of the Knights of Saint John dating back to the year 1107 are now housed in the public library, or *biblioteca*, on Republic Street in Valletta.

lands to block the flow of reinforcements from France. The French were besieged, quickly grew short of food and water, and eventually capitulated.

So it was that the British ended up in control of Malta. Only over time would the British come to realize the enormous strategic value of the islands. At first it was a matter of debate what to do with this new acquisition; there were even plans to return the land to the Order of Saint John. The Maltese, however, had grown disenchanted with the rule of the Knights and preferred that the British remain. This opened a new chapter in Malta's history during which English became a second language to most Maltese and Malta became a symbol of heroism and resilience to the British.

FROM THE SHADOW OF EMPIRE

The British administration of Malta lasted for 164 years and was often an uneasy relationship. The British adopted Malta as a crown colony in 1814. After 1840, as the French flexed their military muscles in the Mediterranean, Britain moved to exploit Valletta's creeks as dockyards and fueling stations. But the value of a Maltese port-of-call extended beyond military expediency — after the Suez Canal was opened in 1869, Malta became one of the principal coaling stations for steamships en route from Britain to India and the Far East. Because of Malta's military importance and its place on this "imperial seaway," it virtually ceased to be an island in the full sense of the word. Malta's value to Britain was retained until the early years of the twentieth century when other Mediterranean ports-of-call, such as Tunis, were developed and began competing.

The onset of World War I failed to bring the prosperity that earlier wars had fostered. In fact, the war caused inflation and other economic distress that provoked a strike by dock workers in 1917 and street riots in 1919. These acts of revolt influenced Britain to give the Maltese a greater say in governing the islands. Although constitutions had been drafted in 1835, 1849, 1887, and 1903 to give the Maltese more influence in running the country, they had limited success. In 1921, Malta was granted self-government in all local affairs. Not surprisingly, it was during the 1920s that the political parties and vigorous alliances for which Malta is well-known today, first emerged.

Self-government did not work well and was twice suspended in the 1930s, generally a period of disquiet and uncertainty for both the Maltese and their colonial rulers. A particularly thorny issue was whether Maltese or Italian should be the official language of instruction in schools, with the tilt towards Italian by the majority Nationalist Party being of particular concern to the British. It was also a delicate matter considering the loyalty of the vast majority of people to the Roman Catholic Church. Adding to the disappointment of the times was the failure of economic initiatives to diversify the economy away from dependency on military projects. However, some of these early attempts, such as tourism planning, were destined to re-emerge much later as powerful economic assets.

Despite the many constitutional and economic problems of the years between the two world wars, this was a period when Malta was starting to make social, political, and economic adjustments to peacetime realities. With rearmament during World War II, however, Malta's structural problems were ignored as it returned to duty as a garrison outpost. The onset of war against Germany and Italy also brought an opportunity in disguise, however, and one that can be linked to Malta's eventual independence and greater self-determination over its economic and political path.

During both world wars, the British government valued Malta primarily for the islands' strategic location, just as so many occupiers had done before. But never before had aerial bombardment played a role in Malta's military history as it would during World War II when the British wartime government decided that Malta would be an effective base from which to attack German and Italian shipping. The plan was to turn the islands into an "unsinkable aircraft

Debris at Tigné from bombing attacks on Malta during World War II.

carrier" as Winston Churchill, the British Prime Minister, phrased it, and from this base sever the lines of supply to the German North Africa campaign. Malta again was caught between warring factions.

By April, 1942, over one thousand ton of bombs per week were being dropped on Malta, and in that same year the islands endured 157 days of continuous aerial raids while supplies of fuel and food ran perilously low. The islands' defense against attacking aircraft was painfully inadequate. Despite the great damage inflicted from the air, there was one remarkable quirk of salvation still keenly remembered today. In the inland town of Mosta there is a massive Christian church with a dome second in size only to Saint Peters Church in Rome. In April, 1942, this dome was pierced by a large German bomb while three hundred worshippers were at prayer. The bomb slid across the floor but failed to explode. This was a deliverance from certain death and destruction that many Maltese still contend was a miracle.

It was also during April, 1942, that King George VI of England awarded the George Cross "for gallantry" to the people of Malta with a citation that can still be recited verbatim by many Maltese. The citation is embedded in the form of a plaque in the wall near the parliament building on Republic Street, Valletta. Another plaque commemorates a citation from Franklin D. Roosevelt, the President of the United States at the time of the siege. Later in 1942, the second Great Siege of Malta was lifted when a convoy of relief supplies limped into Grand Harbor. In October of that year, the Axis powers lost the battle of El Alamein and with it North Africa. In September, 1943, the Commander in Chief of Naval Operations was able to inform London that the Italian fleet had surrendered "under the guns of the fortress of Malta." Today, old gun emplacements, now gone to ruin, are still to be seen in Tigné, near Valletta, and along with the shell of the bombed Opera House, serve as a reminder of grim times gone by.

In September, 1947, the islands once again attained self-government at a time when economic issues were becoming particularly troubling. By 1949, dockyard workers were becoming unemployed and this quickly became a hotly contested political issue. Into the 1950s, surveys and reports on economic development suggested that industry, agriculture, and tourism should be assisted by government grants or building schemes, including plans to convert the Royal Navy dockyard to commercial use. Unfortunately, many of these ideas, including a poorly conceived plan to assemble American cars in Malta under license, proved to be a disappointment. In terms of the shipyard redevelopment, commercial ventures and privatization proved problematic from the outset, and were unprofitable.

The fight to forge a future identity for Malta involved great political rivalry in the post-war years both within Malta and between Maltese political leaders and Britain. There were frequent close elections in 1950, 1951, 1953, and 1955, and switches in government leadership. Only in the election of 1955 did the Maltese Labour Party, led by Dominic Mintoff, obtain a clear electoral majority. It was under Mintoff's leadership that a proposal was made for Malta to become part of

Great Britain, but many groups felt that Malta would lose its identity in such an arrangement. Roman Catholic leaders in Malta were also very uneasy about so close an alliance with a Protestant country. The negotiations between Britain and Malta resulted in tensions on both sides and, following demonstrations in 1958, the constitution was suspended until 1962.

That same year, another hotly contested election brought the Nationalist Party of Giorgio Borg Olivier to power. Significantly, an independence agenda was promoted by both of the major parties in 1962 and was embraced by the majority of the electorate. So it fell to Borg Olivier to propose that for the first time in its long history Malta be granted full independence. There was much debate over this important step, and many felt that the extreme dependence of Malta's tiny economy on Britain precluded the possibility of it ever becoming a viable independent nation-state. Eventually, however, a national referendum was held on the form of the constitution, and Malta achieved independence on September 21, 1964. The terms of independence included a ten-year Mutual Defense Agreement with Britain. This pact brought payment to Malta for the use of the naval dock-yards as needed, and plans for building and redevelopment work so that the final cutoff of military spending would not be abrupt and damaging. Today, just as the United States celebrates Independence Day, so the Maltese have designated September 21 a day of parades and fireworks.

Following independence, Malta be-

The long, narrow, straight streets of Valletta are enhanced and further defined by the many-storied buildings which abut them.

came a member of the British Com-monwealth and, as such, recognized the British Monarch as Head of State. After the country became a republic — *Repubblika Ta' Malta* — in 1974, the

Head of State was the President of Malta. The country now has a one-chamber House of Representatives with sixty-nine members directly elected for five-year terms through a form of proportional representation. There is a fledgling local government structure, but all legislative power is centered in Valletta.

Malta pushed hard for economic diversification in the 1960s and 1970s and this remains an important goal of the Maltese govern-ment. Back then, however, it was very much a race against time to develop sources of revenue and some degree of self-sufficiency be-fore the British mili-tary left. The devel-opment of existing dry-dock facilities and expansion into non-military shipbuilding remained a focus of attention in the 1960s and 1970s, but manufacturing industries, especially textiles, were also encour-aged to take advantage of relatively cheap Maltese labor. In addition, the development of Malta as a center for financial services was also seen as having potential. Malta is developing today as a successful international banking center and exploiting its mid-Mediterranean location as an offshore tax haven.

Unlike many countries in Europe where the church has been stripped of its land holdings, the Roman Catholic Church in Malta is still a prominent landlord. This circumstance, combined with the fact that ninety-eight percent of the Maltese population is Catholic, results in Roman Catholicism occupying a lot of space, both literally and spiritually. The islands constitute a single province of the Catholic Church, and each village in Malta and Gozo is its own parish and is thus a basic territorial unit of the Church. Some larger places, however, may consist of several parishes. Until very recent times there was no separation in Malta between Church and State, and there still is

very little difference between the two in the minds of many Maltese.

Friction between the power of the Church in Malta and others seeking to wield power have been a fact of Maltese life since the time of the Knights, but the level of rivalry has been particularly high in the twentieth century. The Maltese remember vividly, for example, the tension between the Church

Inside Saint Johns Co-Cathedral, Valletta.

and the Maltese Labour Party. This culminated in a 1961 decision by the Church to bolster allegiance to the Archbishop by declaring it a mortal sin to be a Labor Party supporter and to deny the sacraments to all such supporters. Neither was this the first time the Church directly intervened in political affairs wielding such threats. Over the period when the British exercised colonial control they largely understood that it was the Church that controlled the people. Accordingly, the British sought to maintain an effective working relationship with the Archbishop of Malta and the Church. But, in 1927, the Church favored a more pro-Italian political stance than that taken by the ruling political party. The party leader was declared *persona non grata*, and the Church refused absolution to the party's adherents.

The political game has been played with passion in Malta ever since the first breezes of self-determination began to blow in the 1920s. Perhaps it was because the Maltese have been deprived of true independence for hundreds of years that political organization took root so quickly once conditions were favorable. Perhaps, also, it is the powerful vested interests of the Roman Catholic Church and its desire to influence the political course of events. Certainly the parochialism of its village life, where each community has its favored patron saint just as it

has its favored band club and football team, predisposes the people to rivalry. In such a small country, all national issues are also local issues that can soon create divisiveness. In Malta, election campaigns have occasionally been so acrimonious as to cause death and injury. Like the hedges of prickly pear stretched across the Maltese landscape, the political lines become drawn around the thorny issues at the center of Maltese life.

The Labour Party, currently under the leadership of Dr. Alfred Sant, is one of two major parties in Malta, the other being the Nationalist Party, led by the current Prime Minister Edward Fenech-Adami. A small third party with a "green," or pro-environment, agenda also has recently emerged but garnered less than five percent of the vote in the last election. Maltese elections have long been notable for two characteristics — a high turnout and a very close result. In 1992, for example, the voter turnout was 96.1 percent which returned the ruling Nationalist Party to power by a five percent margin over the opposition.

The Nationalist Party, broadly speaking, is committed to the cause of increasing personal and national wealth, minimizing restrictions on private enterprise, and loosening the protectionist economic structure. The Nationalists are also committed to having Malta become a member of the European Union. Since 1987, the Nationalist Party has avoided the confrontational style of socialist governments in office prior to this date and has generally enjoyed a period of peaceful co-existence with the Catholic Church.

For the sixteen years prior to the 1987 elections, the Labour Party held power and followed a largely socialist legislative agenda. The Labour Party emphasized the role of the manual worker and trade unionism in the Maltese economy and believed that key industries should be nationalized. The Labour government constructed a comprehensive welfare state that has helped ensure a high level of health care and social security for the Maltese. The Labour Party also forged close alliances with North African Arab countries and, for a while, Arabic was a compulsory language for school children to learn.

Although there are major differences between a socialist political agenda and a more capitalist one, there is common political ground among the Maltese political parties in at least two fundamental areas. Both parties accept that Malta should remain avowedly neutral in terms of world military alliances and that the welfare state should always remain in place as an important safety

The Labour Party Club in Valletta

net for all Maltese.

For every resident of Malta today, there is one emigrant or descendant living in Australia, Canada, Britain, the United States, or Italy. The Maltese have always been quick to grasp at hope, including opportunities for riches abroad. In this sense, the Maltese played a role in the great wave of European emigration in the early twentieth century. By some estimates, there were two thousand Maltese living in Brooklyn, New York, by 1925. Australia, with its plentiful land and reasonable living costs, was attractive to the Maltese, especially since Australia was actively seeking to increase its population and was prepared to offer travel allowances to would-be settlers. In the late 1940s, growing concerns about overpopulation also lead the Maltese authorities to encourage emigration.

Choosing to leave the islands by no means signified abandonment of Malta. Like many migrants the world over, those that prospered would send money back home to help family, or sometimes as a donation to church causes. The Maltese diaspora, or dispersion, has also helped further expand the strong international perspective of the Maltese. A very simple field experiment in cultural geography in today's Malta would be to walk the streets of a new housing development, where new residents are particularly fond of naming their homes, and see how many house names relate to overseas locations. The result would be surprising! In Zaghra, Gozo, it is traditional to incorporate a carved maple leaf or kangaroo into the stonework of a house to celebrate the link to Canada or Australia.

Today, emigration figures are strikingly different. With ever-increasing prosperity at home and diminished opportunities in the outside world, many former emigrants are coming home. In 1991, one-hundred-forty emigrants left Malta, down from a total of 938 in 1982. But 1991 also saw 1,124 migrants returning home, of whom most were coming from Australia. It now seems unlikely that any government program will again use emigration programs as a means to control population growth since prosperity continues to rise and the domestic demand for labor is strong with a current unemployment rate of about four percent.

NATIONAL SYMBOLS UNITE PAST AND PRESENT

The Maltese Cross, brought to the islands by the Knights of Saint John, contains four arms and eight points. The arms stand for prudence, justice, temperance, and fortitude, while the eight points of the cross represent the Beatitudes as taught in the Sermon on the Mount. When painted or printed, the cross is traditionally white to symbolize purity.

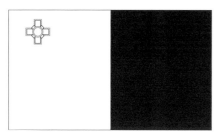

The National Flag of Malta consists of two vertical stripes, equal in area, white on the left and red on the right. The colors and pattern date from the time of Roger the Norman (AD 1090–1194). The George Cross, outlined in red and located in the upper left corner of the white stripe, dates from 1942 when King George VI of England awarded the George Cross to the people of Malta for their bravery and sacrifice during World War II.

The Emblem of Malta consists of a shield representing the national flag. A gold crown situated above the shield represents the fortifications of Malta and denotes a city state. An olive and palm branch, each in its true colors, lie along the left and right side of the shield respectively, and symbolize peace. The branches are tied at the base with a white ribbon, upon which is written the name of the country — Repubblika Ta' Malta — in Maltese.

HARVESTS OF PEACE

It is significant that almost half of this book is given over to the history of Malta because the present-day geography of the islands — whether concerned with the built environment or the human and economic environment — cannot be understood without first understanding the past. Today's Malta is the product of long centuries of colonial domination, invasions, and economic and social adjustment.

The days of military fleets steaming into Valletta's Grand Harbor are now a memory. Malta has known no invading forces since World War II and does not expect any in the foreseeable future. So often caught between warring factions and forced to serve as a fortress outpost for a colonial power, Malta's loss of military importance has required it to adapt to a different world, since its past prosperity often came from war and its short-term economic windfalls.

After so many generations of dependency, what does Malta now offer the world? Certainly, a wealth of human

resources and a population that is well-educated, multilingual, and highly adaptable as a workforce, and that has acquired a keen international perspective. Though geographically isolated, Malta has inherited a remarkably advanced industrial base from its history as a military outpost.

And what does Malta now offer its people? The reshaping of the economic landscape since independence has brought steadily rising levels of prosperity. This in turn has wrought changes to the built landscape from increased residential and industrial construction. The social landscape, also, has changed as bonds between church, family, and village have been loosened. Where the changes of the past thirty years have been most profound, Malta finds itself entering a brave new world. But not all has been changed. Let us now visit the most important of the landscapes of modern Malta and examine them more closely.

Although Malta is one of the most

densely populated countries in the world, you would not know it by walking through its capital city or any of the surrounding towns. There are no high-rise apartment buildings, and though Valletta's Republic Street and adjacent Merchant Street throb with life on weekends, there is little sense of oppressive crowds once you saunter into the side streets with their many flights of stone steps. Population figures can be misleading. Looking behind the numbers to examine the density within urban areas we find a maximum of four hundred persons per square mile, fairly low by comparison with other European urban areas.

Some would say the density is too low, and given the scarcity of land in the islands perhaps some high-rise developments may not be such a bad thing. In the 1980s, government housing schemes provided cheap and sometimes excessively large plots of land on which owners could build. Often this new housing was built outside of existing towns and cities, contributing to a poorly planned sprawl.

The demand for Malta's limited space does not come just from housing, however. There are many essential industrial activities that have to be located somewhere, and these activities are not always in harmony with the environment. Only in the last few years has the government committed to an overall plan for Malta's built environment by commissioning complete studies of land resources and the various interests that compete for space. The situation today sometimes shows an uncomfortable juxtaposition of old building with new. From the ramparts of Mdina, with its twisting alleyways and medieval houses, new housing can be seen encroaching from almost all directions.

To get a sense of the many demands made upon the Maltese landscape, let's take a brief tour. The port town of Marsaxlokk is a good place to start. All bus routes on Malta's main island radiate from the circular bus park outside the city gate of Valletta, from where

Many side streets in Valletta consist of steps, one of the distinguishing characteristics of the capital of Malta.

Marsaxlokk is about a forty-minute trip. After winding its way through the dock area outside Valletta, our lovingly maintained bus, with its characteristic once green, now orange, livery, well-worn forty-year-old seats, and crucifix hanging over the dashboard, has barely reached a stretch of open countryside when it coasts down the last hill before the sea and rolls to a stop on the corner across from the parish church.

It's noon on Sunday and the Angelus bell is ringing to bring the parishioners to prayer. As in many Maltese towns, a twin-belfried church of Italianate style stands high above the well-kept two- or three-story homes. Here, as elsewhere, the church is not only a visual focal point of the town but also the center of local pride. Small shops are interspersed among the homes, but there are no large supermarkets, for Malta is still very much a place of small family businesses serving a local clientele.

Being Sunday, most shops are closed, but numerous small cafes are open for tea, beer, and sandwiches.

Stretched along the quayside for over a quarter-mile are the stalls of the Sunday market. Here we find lace sellers interspersed with fishmongers, tubs of octopus share company with tee-shirts and displays of fresh vegetables brought to market by some of the local part-time farm-

Colorful buses are diligently maintained and provide transportation throughout most of Malta and Gozo.

Pastoral pursuits still endure on Malta, but with an increasing population and intensifying pressures it is not certain how long traditional land uses will continue.

open for tea, beer, and sandwiches.

Stretched along the quayside for over a quarter-mile are the stalls of the Sunday market. Here we find lace sellers interspersed with fishmongers, tubs of octopus share company with tee-shirts and displays of fresh vegetables brought to market by some of the local part-time farmers, and cassette players compete for space with finches chirping in their cages. As if the market's variety were not colorful enough, in the background brightly colored *luzzus*, the local wooden fishing boats, ride at anchor or else have been hauled out and are being sanded down and painted by their fastidious owners. On the prows

of many of the boats are painted eyes that are said, by tradition, to protect the mariners aboard by seeing all evil and warding it away before harm comes.

Walking beyond the market stalls we look out across the water towards Delimara Point and are reminded that the built environment of Malta is far from being all Old-World charm and color. Less than a mile to the southeast, the cliffs have been carved away to make space for a new oil-fired power station. Part of the energy produced goes to power the seawater desalinization plants on which the Maltese so much depend. Where to put

From the hilltop road out along the peninsula, several crude aqueducts can be found, all of which carry valuable rainfall from road surface to field. Also to be seen are hand painted signs on walls reading "RTO." This stands for *reservato*, indicating that the landowner or tenant has designated the area as a private hunting ground. Near these signs we can see a number of small stone platforms on which caged birds are sometimes placed to attract free-flying birds to within shooting range. Looking down as we walk, the number of spent shotgun cartridges attests to the enthusiasm of the shooters.

Beyond the town, to the west of Marsaxlokk, the roads narrow into lanes. On one side of the lane it is mostly the more traditional Maltese homes that we see — very cubic in style with relatively small windows. They are all made of stone, of course. Front doors are often stoutly constructed of wood and heavy wooden window shutters are common. Such homes can be deliciously cool in summer but decidedly chilly in winter when the use of space heaters is common. Roofs are flat and fitted with the obligatory water cistern. Some of the old houses have a bull's skull fastened above the roof with the horns pointing out. Like the painted eyes on the *luzzus*, these horns are traditionally thought to ward away evil. Certainly effective at warding away intruders is another rooftop fixture — the household dog. There always seems to be one to bark insistently at passers-by.

On the other side of the lane there are newer homes, often more starkly white than the older structures and more closely packed together. Where several of the homes are still under construction, limestone blocks are stacked nearby. These blocks are soft enough to be cut with a circular saw, and this is one of the builders' most important tools. Often, new homes in Malta are sold as "shells" which require finishing and fitting out by the new owners. Whether new or old, virtually every home has a television antenna. Programs broadcast from Italy are particularly popular with the Maltese and introduce a potent cultural and linguistic influence into Malta.

Looking out to the southwest between the houses we notice that Saint

Limestone is the primary building material of Malta. Soft and easily worked when fresh, this stone hardens with age and, everywhere, lends a golden tone to the Maltese landscape.

Georges Bay and Pretty Bay have come into view. From our position above sea level we can see a major port development with cranes and container handling facilities to the seaward side of Pretty Bay. Closer in, numerous large containers for liquefied gas, a common source of fuel in Maltese homes and businesses, are competing for space with houses and cropland. What we are seeing with all this development is the end result of one of the government's five-year plans which, in the late 1970s, identified a need for expanded port facilities outside the Valletta area. The port of Marsaxlokk is a "freeport," meaning that no excise taxes are levied on incoming or outgoing goods.

Circling around back towards our starting point we can stand atop a stone wall and count at least three large churches which, like sundials,

Colorful luzzus in the harbor at Gzira, west of Valletta across Marsamxett Harbor.

pass their shadows slowly over their parishes. Regardless of our line-of-sight, religious icons are always present in Malta, either in the form of statuary occupying niches on street corners, or on the scale of the sixteenth-century Saint Johns Co-Cathedral in Valletta (one of the two cathedrals in Malta — the other being in Mdina) with its intricately decorated ceiling and tombs of the Grandmasters. But today's visitor to Malta should look beyond the statuary and architecture that is so much a part of the religious landscape, to gauge the power behind these symbols.

Until very recently, the major divisions of the Maltese day were those rung out by church bells, and the year was divided between religious festivals. Although the days are largely over when the Church ordained a strict code of moral conduct — and sometimes political conduct — the power of the Church as a social force is still very strong. Within the village hierarchy, the parish priest is still a very important person.

If you visit Malta during spring or summer you will notice that there seems to be a lot of marching bands.

Band clubs, whose brassy sound and pseudo-military trappings may be an inheritance from the days of occupation by British colonial forces, are in keen competition with one another and form an important social bond for the people of the various villages and towns. Visitors unfamiliar with the culture of Malta often fail to see the strong links between the bands and the Church. The link is plainest to detect during religious holidays since the bands are especially exuberant during local *festi* which celebrate the particular patron saint of a community and may last several days. During a *festa*, the local church will be handsomely decorated inside and out. In addition, many bands take direct part in religious functions, especially in the period just before Easter.

The best indication that a *festa* has begun, apart from the bands and processions in the streets, is the deafening explosions of fireworks. One of the Maltese words for fireworks, *musketteirja*, means "musket fire." This suggests that, like brass bands, fireworks displays emulate military activities. Thirty different *festi* are celebrated

MALTA'S PUBLIC HOLIDAYS

The nation's public holidays are a good reflection of Malta's historical and cultural geography, particularly its deeply rooted religious identity. Politics are also extremely important to the Maltese and this, too, is reflected in the holiday calendar. In fact, the calendar of holidays depends on the political party in power at the time. Notice the June 7 holiday which celebrates a popular uprising in 1919 by the people against the British authorities in Malta because of price increases that the Maltese felt were intolerable. Note also the Workers' Day, or May Day celebration that reflects the strongly socialist leanings of the Maltese government for much of the country's post-colonial period.

It is important to remember that the Maltese, a devoutly Catholic people, are always eager to celebrate a saint's special day with parades and fireworks. So, in addition to the public holidays listed here, there are a number of additional feast days in the calendar, including Carnival, held the week before Lent; the Feast of Saint John the Baptist, on June 24; and the Feast of Our Lady of Sorrows, held in Valletta on the Friday before Palm Sunday. Christmas festivities in Malta have not yet been heavily commercialized and remain family-centered celebrations.

January 1	New Year's Day
February 10	Saint Paul's Shipwreck
March 19	Feast of Saint Joseph
March 31	Freedom Day
Variable	Good Friday/Easter
May 1	Workers' Day
June 7	Commemoration of June 7, 1919
June 29	Feast of Saint Peter and Saint Paul
August 15	Feast of the Assumption
September 8	Feast of Our Lady of Victories
September 21	Independence Day
December 8	Feast of the Immaculate Conception
December 13	Republic Day
December 25	Christmas Day

each year. On the main island, the *festa* of the saints Peter and Paul, celebrated on June 29, is accompanied by family picnics in the grove of trees at Buskett, south of Rabat, and horse racing or water sports. Everywhere, *festi* are rowdy affairs and an excuse for family and friends to have fun. The original

Narrow streets are filled to overflowing during the Festa of Saint Helen.

festi were simple affairs often involving the giving of charity to the poor. Today, these lavish spectacles, because of the interest of tourists, seem to grow more exuberant and more numerous each year. The success of a *festa* now depends to a large extent on the amount of financial contributions received.

In past times the *festa* was also an opportunity for unmarried men and women to get together, but now dating follows much more the familiar European style. With the growth of tourism, and with it places to go dancing or find other fun at the resort areas, there are plenty of social opportunities for the young. Perhaps because the country's history has been so intertwined with foreign peoples, there is little social segregation between the Maltese and

visitors from elsewhere, although in private moments they will admit to having preferences.

There are no major differences in marrying age for the Maltese when compared to those marrying in the United States or elsewhere in Europe. Of the 2,541 marriages in 1991, for example, most of the men who married were between twenty-five and twenty-nine, while the women were mostly between the ages of twenty and twenty-four. Marriage is often put off for a few years in order to put some extra money aside or else to make sure that everything is provided to set up a household, and this is an increasingly common decision as more single women enter the labor force. Perhaps only baptisms can really compare with marriages as social occasions. Certainly both are festive affairs, but marriages are more socially complex because they represent not just a commitment between two people, but also the melding of two extended families with all the associated issues of prestige and status.

Another revealing exercise that can be done in Malta is to walk through the streets of Valletta or any of the larger towns and note the names over the doorways of the little neighborhood stores. Do you notice how so many names recur? There are relatively few family names in Malta. Farrugia, Mifsud, Vella, and Micallef are particularly common names, and each family includes many relatives. Social contacts were once confined to specific villages and towns, but the Maltese social horizon now extends well beyond such confines.

This expanded horizon has resulted from changing patterns and means of communication. In terms of personal transportation, for example, there is now one car to every three people. The effects of increased car ownership on social contacts among the Maltese might well have caused a lessening of identification with one's home town.

Certainly the phenomenon of car as social status symbol has arrived. On a weekend, the narrow roads on the north side of the main island between Saint Pauls Bay and Saint Julians are often jammed with families on car outings en route to a picnic site, taking in the views that they must have seen countless times before. Some years ago the prospect of building a bridge between Malta and Gozo was seriously considered. Though the plan was shelved because of cost, the thought of the additional traffic released onto the country lanes of Gozo is rather alarming. Social visits between islanders now depend on the car ferry service or a bus-to-ferry connection. There is also a helicopter service for those really in a hurry.

Another example of communications change is in access to media, particularly television, now a status symbol just like the family car. But along with that attraction comes the possibility of change to social patterns and social values. There seems now less conversation in the clubs and bars of the villages as heads are turned to watch an Italian television program. By comparison, it is reassuring when one occasionally comes across a late afternoon game of *bocci* being played on a sandy court with the traditional barrel-shaped ball, the players engrossed with each others' play and remarks. Notice, though, the age of the bowlers. Sixty? Seventy? Older perhaps? Will the young of the future also find equal pleasure in the oaken thunk of a *bocci* ball?

Certainly the comparison between the game of *bocci* and the playing of the political game is a stark one. With the latter, there is no sign that the old earnestness is in any way changing. Still a social fixture in many larger villages and towns is the local Labour Party Club. To turn a political party headquarters into a social club, often open to tourists, seems odd to many visitors,

but to the Maltese this melding of ideology with drinking, laughter, and storytelling comes naturally. As elections draw near, however, the sense of purpose in the air becomes much more plain because, as explained earlier, Maltese politics can be a deadly serious affair.

Another revealing place to see the Maltese blend of merriment and sense of purpose is the local restaurant. With rising levels of income and increased choice of eating places and food, the Maltese have become keen restaurant-goers. Weekend visits to a restaurant are family affairs and it is not unusual to see tables pushed together and chairs shuffled to fit in all the family. The conversation becomes so animated sometimes that it seems almost an in-

A game of bocci, *one of the many fading traditions of Malta.*

terruption when the waiter brings out the plates!

Manufacturing and tourism are the two biggest contributors to Malta's economy today, with manufacturing accounting for about thirty percent of the country's gross domestic product (GDP) and tourism accounting for approximately twenty-seven percent. Malta has less than a dozen sandy beaches, but diving is a common tourist activity as is sailing. On dry land, the resort casinos always draw a crowd. Cultural and historical tourism is also being promoted in Malta focussing on archeology and the fine church and military architecture. Valletta itself has been designated a World Heritage Site by the United Nations.

Important manufacturing industries are textiles, construction, electronics, beverages, and tobacco. As discussed earlier, shipbuilding and ship repair remain important parts of Malta's economic picture. Although the number of full-time farmers has declined, Malta is self-sufficient in native grown potatoes, cauliflower, grapes, tomatoes, and citrus fruits and these are all abundant in the local shops. Overall, however,

Malta produces only twenty percent of the food it needs. This is not a new situation for Malta since grain imports for bread-making have been essential for at least four hundred years. In recent years, the demand for locally caught fish also has outstripped supply. Part of the explanation is that there are fewer than fourteen hundred fishermen left in Malta, of which fewer than two-hundred-fifty work full-time at the trade. Also, the local seas to which these fishermen are restricted are not as abundant in fish as one might think.

To complete the picture of Malta's present day economy we must include another important activity: employment in government. In 1989, over forty-five percent of the work force was employed in government in some form. This is a high figure but perhaps not surprising given that about fifty percent of the economy still remained under government control in 1989. Government functions are strongly centralized and based exclusively in Valletta or the city's very close suburbs such as Floriana. Very few government agencies are fully computerized as yet.

Income for working Maltese has risen

A TASTE OF MALTA

Malta may have found its independence from Britain more than thirty years ago, but its cooking is still trying to shake off the British culinary influence. However, it is not difficult to find authentic Maltese food, and the best place to start is with the little neighborhood stores that have been mentioned earlier. Look for places known as *pastizzeria* which sell *pastizzi*, sometimes called "cheese-cakes." *Pastizzi* are small, cheap, incredibly filling triangular pockets of flaky pastry filled with either mashed peas or ricotta cheese. (They say the best cheese *pastizzi* are salted with seawater, but who knows for sure?) It is common for the Maltese to buy a dozen or more *pastizzi* at a time to take home and everyone, including the author of this book, has a favorite place to buy them. A sweet relative of *pastizzi* that should also be tried are *mqaret*, deep-fried pastries with a date filling that always seem to taste best when bought from a street vendor and eaten outdoors.

The neighborhood mini-markets are also good places to pick up Maltese goat cheese called *gbenja* — small, sand-castle shaped, and just about bite-sized. The ones with a dusting of ground pepper are especially good when eaten with the local stuffed olives, and make a perfect picnic. For dessert you can't beat the fresh-picked local oranges that often have their leaves attached. Compared to the uniform shapes and sizes of vegetables in American and European supermarkets, Maltese vegetables are displayed still muddy from the fields and in a variety of odd shapes and sizes but all with excellent flavor.

Bread is another delight that can be had directly from the local baker so long as you go early in the day. All the breads are very crusty on the outside because

steadily since the country's independence. In 1995, the average weekly wage was fifty-five Maltese liri which is the equivalent of about 185 dollars in the United States. Of course, many professionals earn far more than this. As in other geographic regions, an increasing number of women are in the workforce; almost thirty percent of women currently work outside the home in Malta, compared to just fifteen percent in 1963.

Given that Malta has a number of natural advantages as a tourist destination, it is rather surprising that tourism, as a planned economic activity, only became firmly established in the late 1960s. Here was a country that, despite occasional tensions during the colonial era, was viewed affectionately by the

they are baked directly on the oven surface. They contain no preservatives and should be eaten the same day. The Maltese particularly enjoy *hobz biz-zejt* — bread soaked with olive oil and garnished with tomatoes. The local cakes and pastries should also be eaten fresh and, since the Maltese have quite a sweet tooth, there is always a good selection to be found. The hoop-shaped "honey rings" are available just about everywhere and are definitely worth trying.

There are no real Maltese national dishes, but particular favorites include rabbit (*fenek*) and an abundant local fish, similar to a dorado, called a *lampuka*. Rabbit is prepared in many forms from deep fried to baked in a pie, while *lampuki* (plural of *lampuka*) are served grilled or fried. As one would expect in a country in such a geographic position as Malta, the culinary tastes of neighboring countries also show through in the menus of local restaurants. Pizza grows more popular each year, and pasta is gaining in popularity but far less is eaten than in nearby Italy.

Of course no tour of the Maltese table would be complete without mentioning that most Mediterranean of accompaniments to all meals, whether a simple picnic, a family dinner at home, or a special occasion in a restaurant — wine. The Maltese have an inferiority complex about their wine, perhaps because of the reputation of the vintages from Italy. Nonetheless, it is entirely enjoyable if undistinguished, and very inexpensive. In addition to basic dry whites and reds, there is a local Sauternes. To some, the wines from Gozo are preferable to those produced on the main island. Many Maltese are enthusiastic amateur vintners, and a chance to sample a home-made bottle should not be passed up since one is being offered not only wine, but also friendship.

British, who represented a huge number of potential tourists. English was widely spoken in Malta, and the dependable sunshine offered welcome relief from the grey skies of northern Europe. In addition, the tradition of service stemming from generations as a fortress outpost catering to foreign forces was easily reoriented to tourists. Other attempts at economic diversification into manufacturing industries in the 1960s and 1970s have had only mixed success, so tourism has been eagerly embraced as the best and brightest hope for a secure economic future.

The Maltese government has moved quickly to foster hotel building schemes and to bring island roads, electricity supply, and airport facilities up to a

Tourist Arrivals in Malta, 1960–1994

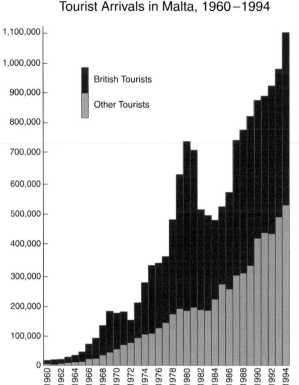

complaints. The large dip in tourism after 1980 cannot be wholly attributed to water problems, however. There were ugly political disturbances in Malta following the 1981 elections, and acts of terrorism, unrelated to Malta, were taking place elsewhere in the Mediterranean region during this time.

Tourism figures have revived since 1984, and it has become clear that tourism represents the latest and greatest wave of invasion this much invaded land has experienced. Just as the walls of Valletta, Mdina, and Victoria were raised in response to foreign landings, so the rising walls of the new tourism facilities along Malta's northern coastline are the response to the islands' most recent arrivals. With more than one million tourists arriving annually, there is a growing sense that the ceiling has been reached. Now the government tourist organization is switching its attention away from counting numbers in favor of encouraging those tour-

more modern standard. Through the late 1970s, things seemed to be working reasonably well and there was a sharp rise in tourist arrivals. However, economic aims are tied to physical geography and the course of political events, and the sensitivity of tourism to negative events became clear around 1980. Beginning in the early 1980s, the lack of a dependable high-quality water supply compared unfavorably to conditions back home and caused many

ists with more specialized interests who, though perhaps fewer in number, will spend more when they visit.

Water supply has been a problem throughout much of the islands' history, and the Maltese are quick to remark that they never get rain when they need it. Although much vegetation lies dormant during the summer months because of the low soil mois-

ture, summer activity beyond the fields is anything but dormant, for that is the time when tourists descend upon Malta. This seasonal surge of visitors, who outnumber residents three-to-one, places additional demands on the water supply exactly at the time that rainfall is at its minimum.

Until the 1980s, there were two ways to obtain water in Malta — to trap rainwater or to drill wells into the underground aquifer. As the lower aquifer, located at sea level, was increasingly exploited to meet growing demand, it became more and more depleted. So severe had this depletion become by 1980 that seawater was be-

Malta's growing tourism industry is based on water and sun. Diving is important, but sailing, windsurfing, swimming, hiking, cultural festivities, gambling — and golf — among other activities, are available.

ginning to intrude into the fresh water supply. Clearly the government had to act to prevent water shortages from disrupting development plans. Seawater distillation — extracting fresh water from salt water — had been tried and abandoned in the late 1960s due to the high energy costs involved. Now the

The marina and hotels welcome tourists at Saint Julians on the north coast of Malta.

government re-examined the options and a decision was made to re-invest in desalinization technology. A plant was built in the south of the main island at Ghar Lapsi and began operating, with great effectiveness, in 1983. Spurred by this success, other plants were built, the latest one being commissioned in 1992. Today, the Maltese depend upon desalinization technology for over fifty percent of their daily supply of fresh water. The demand continues to rise as economic development, including tourism, expands to create a seemingly unquenchable thirst.

To turn the faucet in Malta is thus to participate in a brave experiment.

There is a limit to how much reliance can be placed on seawater desalinization and a point beyond which costs outweigh benefits, but no one can yet tell what those limits are. Overall energy costs are a major concern and desalinization accounts for almost twenty percent of all electricity generated in Malta. Since Malta has no energy resources of its own, all of its fuel must be imported. Since desalinization consumes much fuel, the Maltese are, in a sense, drinking imported water.

The natural environment of Malta has been under pressure ever since the islands first became heavily settled, but never has that pressure been felt as acutely as at the end of the twentieth century. The reason is the country's economic development and the building that has occurred as a result. The land area occupied by buildings increased from just five percent in 1957 to sixteen percent in 1985. Agricultural land decreased from fifty-six percent in 1957 to less than thirty-eight percent by 1985. Some previously open land also disappeared beneath new roadways.

old ways of planting and harvesting are disappearing rapidly. As late as 1985, it was possible to sit on virtually any stone wall in rural Malta and, squinting through the bright sunshine of an autumn morning, watch a farmer till the soil with a horse-drawn plow. That is a rare sight today due to the great popularity and relatively low cost of rototillers. Rare also now is that quintessentially Mediterranean scene of shepherd and flock.

The desalinization plant at Ghar Lapsi provides some of Malta's much-needed water.

Even though the land may not be buried entirely beneath roads and buildings, the simple abandonment of agriculture as a way of life represents a great cultural loss. Between 1956 and 1991, the number of full-time farmers declined by eighty percent. Part-time farming remains very important but the

Not only is the agrarian way of life in danger of disappearing, but also the fundamental resource that sustained that way of life — the soil. Much agricultural land is on sloping ground and terraced with stone walls. Once these stone walls become neglected, the soil they retain is quickly washed away by the winter rains. Considering how scarce fertile soils are on Malta and how laboriously protected they have been in the past, this would be a tragic loss.

Despite their limited size, the islands support some very rare species of fauna and flora. There are twenty-one species of flowering plants, twenty-five of beetles, seventeen of mollusks, and the same number of moths and butterflies that are found nowhere else in the world. One species of Maltese orchid, *Ophrys oxyrrhynchos,* has already been rendered extinct by the stone quarrying industry, and there is great concern that loss of habitat will condemn other species to a similar fate. Rare residents are found not only on the land but also above it — there are fifty-seven types of birds that visit regularly and one-hundred-twelve migrants that use Malta as a stopover on their north-south journeys. It is particularly tragic that Maltese men will traditionally shoot any passing bird that appears at all exotic. By so doing, they dramatically increase the threat to birds already badly affected by increasing development of the island landscape. Particularly poignant, because of their historical symbolism, is the case of the Maltese peregrine falcons. Until the late 1980s, these still nested in Malta until the last breeding pairs were shot. Fortunately, such behavior is now being increasingly criticized in Maltese newspapers and in the international media and hopefully this will eventually change attitudes. Additional positive steps are the designation of protected areas, such as Salina Bay in the north of the main island, and the clifftop area of Fungus Rock in western Gozo. Also, now that the bombs no longer fall upon it, the tiny island of Filfa has a more positive and humane use as a bird sanctuary. It remains to be seen how rigorously the new laws designed to protect wildlife are enforced.

FINDING SPACE FOR TOMORROW

To stand on a street corner in a suburb of Valletta ten years ago was to take a step back in time as a parade of aging cars, kept running by the ingenuity of back-street mechanics, passed by. Stand on that same corner today and many cars that pass will be new. In many ways, the view from that street corner provides a realization of the challenges ahead for this small island nation. Far beyond the fact that along with those new cars must come new roads is the need for a broader appraisal of how the Maltese will cope with growing prosperity and expanding expectations, solve the dilemma of providing space for an expanding population, and maximize use of a truly precarious natural resource base.

History has dealt a lean hand to Malta, but there are many indications that important lessons have been learned that will serve the country well in the future. Because of its history, Malta is keenly aware of the importance of economic, political, and cultural alliances. The memory remains strong of the false prosperity that can come from military activities on its soil, perhaps explaining why Malta, a member of the United Nations since 1964, has had a non-alignment policy since

As Malta's human population increases and pressures for residential and commercial building intensify, the islands' traditional landscapes are being transformed. Here, new houses and the Marsaxlokk power plant stand alongside terraced and fenced fields.

1987. Ever since approaches were made to the European Union for a formal relationship, it has been clear that Malta's sense of geographical kinship lies to its north. Malta has been actively pursuing full membership in the European Union since 1990, and seventy percent of Malta's trade is with the member states, but by the latest assessment it will be several years before Malta is admitted to full membership.

Other foundation stones for future success were also laid in the past, such as commitment to democratic political ideals, an emphasis on the importance of education, and equal access to health care. The homogeneity of the Maltese population makes for a relatively coherent sense of identity — there is the one official language of *Malti* plus the widespread use of English, one religion, and one cultural heritage. Personal expectations are, for the most part, made very clear — loyalty to family is considered basic; education is valued and compulsory until the age of sixteen; voting in important elections is expected. On the other hand, some might question the social restrictions that Maltese society carries with it into the future. Divorce, for example, is illegal, as is abortion. The lack of ethnic diversity means that the social creativity that stems from multiculturalism is not to be found in Malta. Some might also question the factionalism that Maltese loyalty can involve. Political rivalry creates the danger that animosities might again cripple government agendas, causing social divisions and economic dislocation, as they have in the past.

Because of the very small land area of the Maltese Islands, the issue of space will be one of the most pressing in the years ahead. In fact, it would be hard to find another country whose future will hinge so much on the interrelationship between economics and land area. The stated aim of the present government is to increase national wealth; it is inevitable that open land will be lost in the process of development. But which land, and how much should be sacrificed? One of the more important government documents of the last five years is the *Structure Plan for the Maltese Islands* which attempts to lay out an agenda for the

MEET THE FARRUGIAS — A MALTESE FAMILY

Joseph and Annie Farrugia live in Rabat, a ten-minute walk from the old walled city of Mdina in central Malta. They have two daughters, Nathalie and Marija, and one son, Paul. Nathalie, now twenty-three, works for *Air Malta*, the state airline, where her fluency in English, Arabic, and Italian is an asset. Her sister, twenty-one, is a nurse at Saint Luke's, one of several major hospitals in Malta. Paul, twenty-six, worked for four years in the government's Public Works Department but has recently been promoted to a position in the Ministry for Development of Infrastructure. "Things are really hectic now, what with all the new planning regulations," says Paul. Marija is the only one not married, but she has been engaged for a year and is saving money to help furnish the nearby new home which Joe and Annie are buying for her. Just like Paul and Nathalie, Marija will be marrying someone she first met from the local high school, even though the boys and girls had segregated classes. Annie became a grandmother last year when Paul's wife Taziana had a baby boy. Nathalie wants to start a family but worries about maintaining her career.

Joe and Annie live on the ground floor of a two-story, seventy-year-old terrace house with Marija. Joe's mother, recently widowed, lives upstairs. "Before all the new building out back you could see out across the fields," Joe recalls. He is particularly proud of the large garage next to the house where he maintains his 1968 English Austin. "The neighbors say I should buy a new car, but this one seems like part of the family." Joe drives it to his job with the Post Office in Valletta every day. Annie walks to her job as housekeeper and receptionist at a local hotel. Joe also helps out there part-time when it gets busy in the summer. Between them, they earn the equivalent of $11,000 US per year. In addition to their home in Rabat, Joe and Annie have inherited from Joe's father an old stone farmhouse in Xlendi, Gozo. They have converted the ground floor, where the farm animals used to feed, into a kitchen and they now rent the property to tourists in the summer. "Ten years ago, the old place didn't seem worth much, but now they tell me I could sell it for over 50,000 liri. Crazy! But we'll keep it in the family because the yearly income is welcome."

Asked about the future, Joseph and Annie Farrugia are optimistic. "We never really have a holiday," says Annie. "Once every three or four years I visit cousins in England, but Joe has never left Malta." "We enjoy being here and working hard for the children and grandchildren," explains Joe. "Our worries? Taxes, yes. And the cost of living. But, all-in-all, life is good. Now, before you go, you must have a peacake and try some of our home-made wine...."

geographic and economic challenges of the future. One idea for rationalizing land use is to build a regional shopping center, but what then would happen to the many small neighborhood shops that are such an important part of the community fabric? The plan also discusses the possibility of an "arterial network" of roads, but will that not simply attract more cars and pollution and pave over more scarce island land? There are no easy answers.

Challenges of the years ahead are made more difficult by Malta's increasing population. Since the beginning of the twentieth century, the population of the Mediterranean region as a whole has increased over fourfold. The population of Malta is expected to reach over 377,000 by the year 2010, a 15.7 percent increase over the figure for 1985 when the last census was taken. There is no denying that increasing

population numbers, coupled with increased prosperity, will translate into ever greater pressure on land and water resources and increased energy use. Ever since its last tree was axed for fuel, Malta has been without its own fuel resources. Despite the relative abundance of oil reserves beneath the seabed south of Sicily and to the north of Libya, extensive drilling beneath Maltese waters has brought nothing but dry wells and frustration. In January, 1994, one of the two major multinational companies drilling beneath Malta's seas decided to cease operations, much to the disappointment of

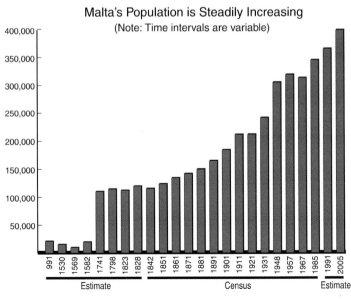

Malta's Population is Steadily Increasing
(Note: Time intervals are variable)

the Maltese government. One future alternative to dependence on fossil fuels such as oil and coal may be solar power; there is certainly no shortage of sunshine in Malta. Wind power is another possible alternative.

Despite much being said and written about the population density of Malta, a sound case can be made that Malta is not, and will not become, an overpopulated island. Indeed, it is likely that Malta will shortly follow the demographic trends evident in other Mediterranean countries, such as Italy, where population growth has virtually ceased. Though it is true that people use basic resources such as land, energy, and water, we must also remember that people are a basic resource in their own right and, in the case of Malta, which has few resources in the usual sense, a productive and adaptable population is perhaps its best resource of all.

Fort Saint Elmo at the northeast end of Valletta stands as veteran and symbol of Malta's history of endurance and adaptability.

GEOGRAPHICAL MILESTONES

in Maltese History

3800	Neolithic farmers present in Malta; agriculture, permanent settlement, and temple-building known from this period.
700	Phoenicians used Malta as stopping-point on Mediterranean trade routes; roots of *Malti* language probably introduced at this time.
218 BC	Malta came under the administration of Rome.
AD 60	According to the Bible, Saint Paul shipwrecked on Malta; conversion of Maltese to Christianity began.
870	Arabs invaded and occupied Malta; brought Islam and agricultural reforms.
1090	Roger the Norman invaded Malta; reestablished European domination of islands.
1530	Islands ceded to Knights of Saint John by Charles V of Spain, followed by much new construction and increases in population and wealth.
1565	Knights defeated invading Ottoman Turks to end Great Siege.
1798	Invasion by French under Napoleon Bonaparte; Knights ousted.
1800	French expelled, Malta fell under protection of Britain.
1814	Malta became British Crown Colony.
1914–1918	Malta used as military garrison and hospital during World War I.
1917	Strike by dockyard workers over worsening economic conditions.
1921	Self-government in domestic affairs began for first time; political alliances began to appear.
1936	*Malti* designated official language of courts; English became language of administration.
1939–1945	Malta used as military garrison and base of operations against Germany and Italy during World War II.
1942	Second Great Siege; Britain awarded Malta George Cross for bravery.
1959	First five-year development plan published.
1964	Malta became independent nation, but remained within British Commonwealth; economic diversification encouraged.
1974	Malta became republic; President replaced British Monarch as Head of State.
1979	Last British forces left Malta.
1983	First desalinization plant placed in operation at Ghar Lapsi.
1990	Malta applied for membership in European Union; *Structure Plan for the Maltese Islands* published.
1994	Tourism arrivals exceeded one million for the first time.

Sources of

ADDITIONAL INFORMATION

LITERATURE

Blouet, Brian. 1972. *The Story of Malta.* London: Faber and Faber.

Boissevain, Jeremy. 1965, 1993. *Saints and Fireworks. Religion and Politics in Rural Malta.* Valletta, Malta: Progress Press.

Bradford, Ernle. 1961. *The Great Siege: Malta 1565.* Harmondsworth, Middlesex: Penguin Books.

Eadie, Peter McGregor. 1990. *Blue Guide: Malta and Gozo, Third Edition.* New York: W. W. Norton.

Fox, Robert. 1993. *The Inner Sea. The Mediterranean and its People.* New York: Knopf.

Hughes, Quentin. 1969. *Fortress: Architecture and Military History in Malta.* London: Lund Humphries.

Malone, Caroline; Anthony Bonanno; Tancred Gouder; Simon Stoddart; and David Trump. 1993. "The Death Cults of Prehistoric Malta." *Scientific American,* vol. 269, no. 6, pp. 110–117.

Sire, H. J. A. 1993. *The Knights of Malta.* New Haven: Yale University Press.

IMPORTANT ADDRESSES

Malta Mission to the United Nations
249 East 35th Street
New York, New York 10016
Telephone 212-725-2345

Embassy of Malta and Consulate General
2017 Connecticut Avenue, NW
Washington, DC 20008
Telephone 202-462-3611

Malta National Tourist Office
249 East 35th Street
New York, New York 10016
Telephone 212-213-6686

MALTA

at a Glance

Official Name	Malta
Derivation of the Name	Probably derived from the Phoenician word *maleth,* meaning "safe haven."
Short Name	Malta
Official Flag	Two vertical bars, red on right and white on left, with George Cross in upper left corner of white bar.
National Anthem	*Lil Din L-Art Helwa* ("To This Sweet Land")
Term for Citizens	Maltese
Area	122 square miles
Population	340,549 (1985 census); 361,000 (1995 estimate)
Percent Urban	85
Official Language	Malti
National Capital	Valletta
Most Populous City	Birkirkara
Currency	Maltese Lira, also known as the Maltese Pound (approximately .35 lira = 1 dollar US in 1995)
Mean Annual Income	Per capita GNP = $8,136 US (1994)
Dominant Ethnic Group	Maltese (>99%)
Dominant Religion	Roman Catholicism (98% of population)
Major National Holidays	January 1 (New Year's Day); March 31 (Freedom Day); Good Friday; May 1 (May Day); August 15 (Assumption of Our Lady); September 21 (Independence Day); December 8 (Immaculate Conception); December 13 (Republic Day); December 25 (Christmas Day).